Endorsements for *Inside Out: the Story Behind the Vision*

I have known Luke for many years. Luke has a call of God on his life to pioneer works and has a passion to reach out and help the lost and hurting. He has wisdom beyond his years and a heart of humility and honour towards God and men. A radical lover of Jesus who is truly laying down his life for others. Luke's life and story is a powerful testimony of the saving grace of God.

Billy Lummis

In the years that I have known and worked with Luke Selway, I have no doubt that God has first saved Luke, given him a burning and unwavering vision, has prepared him through his own life experiences and has equipped him to make a mighty difference in the lives of those whose lives are being destroyed through addiction. His testimony is proof of the power and love of Christ today to entirely change a ruined life into one that is a blessing to others, and that brings glory to God.

Peter Thorne

I work for Green Pastures, a national Christian charity that work with local churches and charities to house homeless people all over the country. I first met Luke in early 2015. I was immediately struck by his fierce determination to make a difference in people's lives and how his faith in Jesus was central to all that he did.

He then told me his story, which is featured in this book. I would challenge anyone, whether they have a faith or not, to not be moved by his story of how hope came out of complete and utter despair, the type of despair that sucks the wind out of you and demands that you give up because everything is futile. Well, that is not how Luke's story ends, praise God, and now Luke is passionately determined to bring the hope that he found to help bring new life to others. Hope is the fuel that now runs Luke's life and it could be yours too. I challenge you to read this story and not be changed by what you read.

Green Pastures are really excited to be working with Luke's charity Inside Out so that we can see people coming off the streets and their lives being transformed by having a home and support. God bless.

Carl Good, Green Pastures

Luke holds no punches in his writing; telling it as it is. This book will inspire those struggling with addiction that there is hope and will challenge those working alongside them that unconditional love has the power to transform a person from the inside out!

Steve Carey, pastor of Family Church Havant and Trustee of Inside Out

INSIDE OUT

INSIDE OUT

THE STORY BEHIND THE VISION

LUKE SELWAY

Published in 2015 by Great Big Life Publishing
Empower Centre, 83-87 Kingston Road, Portsmouth, PO2 7DX, UK

The right of Luke Selway to be identified as the author of this work has been asserted by him
in accordance with the Copyright, Designs and Patents Act 1988.

British Library Cataloguing in Publication Data

A catalogue record for this book is available from the British Library

ISBN-13: 978-09932693-4-9
ISBN-10: 0993269346
eBook ISBN: 978-09932693-5-6

Contents

Dedication

I would like to dedicate this book to God. It is a demonstration of His power and purpose in my life and therefore I want Him to receive all the glory for what He has done and continues to do in my life. It is God who set me free from the terror that my life had become, and it is He who continues to work through me to impact the lives of His people that are so often disqualified by society and, sadly, even His Church.

There are some people I would like to also mention at this point. Firstly, my amazing wife Kudzi, who has stood by me, moved with the vision God has given without question, prayed relentlessly and so often laying her life aside to help with the work of Inside Out. She is a true representation of Proverbs chapter 31 and I am thankful to God that He has joined us together to run this race.

Secondly, I would like to thank the leadership teams of Family Church and Millennium Harvest Church, who have supported the work of Inside Out both in Portsmouth and in Hull. Without the sound advice, support and love of these people I am not sure that Inside Out would have been established.

Lastly, to Peter Thorne, a humble and generous man who is completely in love with God. He has shown me that even when I am old in years, I can still run hard after God. Just because we age doesn't mean we have to become a spectator to the life of His Church.

These people have helped to hold me up when I've felt weak, encouraged, challenged and pushed me to press further into God's love. They've invested in my life and into the vision of Inside Out. It is Jesus who runs through the centre of every one of these relationships. It is Jesus who leads us on.

It is JESUS!

Foreword

I first met Luke during a weekend prayer in our church a few years ago after he had visited family who are members of our church. Our relationship that is centred on loving and serving Christ and others developed since. In the process of time, Luke felt led by Christ's Spirit to relocate to Hull and be part of and serve both in our community and the church, together with his wife Kudzi

In the time I have known him, both as a fellow Christian and his ministry leader (pastor), I have found Luke to have a big heart for seeing people come to the Know and accept Christ. His life story of how Christ saved him and restored his life from the trap of drug addition motivates in him a specific life-purpose. Luke lives to impact those who are in the same circumstance that he was freed from. He has a passion and desire to demonstrate that Christ died for and loves everyone (John 3:16), and that He has the power to release people from the trap of negatively impacting lifestyles and habits such as drug addiction.

I was delighted to learn that Luke was putting his life story into a book. Although Luke has shared his life story with me in person, the book has elaborated it in greater detail. The book gives a more detailed and thorough account of this wonderful testimony. I am confident that many people from all walks of life will find this book enlightening and inspiring. Above all, the book shows how Christ can turn around a life from a state of hopelessness, to one of hope.

It is my prayer and hope that Luke maintains the passion and zeal that he has demonstrated in serving both the Lord, and others.

Hartness Samushonga, Senior Leader,
Millennium Harvest Church, Hull, UK

Chapter 1

The Early Years

I was born on 8th February 1987 in St Mary's Hospital in Portsmouth, England. I was born prematurely and with a kidney infection that was to go unnoticed for two years, the result of which was that my left kidney didn't grow or function very well. I was the youngest of seven children and grew up in a household with my parents and the youngest of my three sisters, my other siblings all living nearby. Both my parents had been married before, my mother having had three children and my father two prior to their marriage.

We lived in a working class household. My mother was a secretary in the Ministry of Defence. My father was a salesman and travelled the world with his job. He would be away for months at a time, and when he was home, he spent a lot of time sleeping and at the pub, so we grew up without a strong father figure. But we lived fairly comfortably, and were well clothed and fed for the most part.

My father drank alcohol most days for as long as I can remember. At the age of five I would be getting him bottles of ale from the fridge. My mother would work long hours, probably to help make ends meet as the majority of my father's wage would go towards footing his tab at the local establishment.

To help my mother, a close family friend (who, for the purposes of this book, we shall call Ben) would look after me at weekends. My mother would sometimes give me money to go to the cinema or to the shops – anything to keep me occupied. I never did get to do those things. Instead Ben and his mates would pocket the cash and take me out 'adventuring', as they called it. 'Adventuring' involved me being posted through open windows and unlocking the front door in various properties. I was told not to touch anything but to look for anything valuable.

Although this sounds a little like *Oliver Twist* and is obviously totally immoral, at the age of five, when someone seventeen years older than you, who you and your family trusts, tells you something is OK, you don't ask questions.

This pattern continued and, as time went on, I was trusted to go on 'solos'. This was where I was given the address and sent alone to break in while Ben and his friends went 'to see a man about a dog'. I didn't really know what this meant, but I actually quite enjoyed the feeling of trust and being one of the lads. I didn't want to let them down.

Around this time my father lost his job due to his drinking habits infringing upon his employment, so my parents came up with a great way to put food on the table. They told us they had spoken to the manager of the local supermarket and prepaid for our food and that we were to go and collect it. We were given a list and sent on our way. In we would go to fill the trolley with the various items on the list and, once this was done, we'd just walk out. It amazes me to this day that not once were we stopped or asked where our parents were.

I was still regularly attending school at this point, with my 'extracurricular activities' taking place after school. This, however, was all about to change. At age six I began to be bullied. I was very short for my age, had severe eczema and was behind with my education. I could not read and my teacher didn't have time to teach me, saying I was hard work and would never get it. I was just given extra playtime and left with part of a Meccano set and some jigsaw puzzles with missing pieces.

Now it doesn't take a rocket scientist to know that, put in this position, a child with an active mind gets very bored very quickly. The boredom of class, coupled with the torment of the bullies who would punch, kick, spit at me and call me names, caused me to decide to just stop going to school. Besides, I didn't get this aggravation from my friends outside of school.

So from the age of six my attendance at school was patchy to say the least. I would go to Ben's flat and continue 'adventuring'. By age seven I was an accomplished thief. I knew what I was doing was wrong now, but the feeling of inclusion was all I knew in the way of love. I was out of control, going to new extremes to impress my friends. We would steal from shops, businesses, homes and cars. I also became a dab-hand at pick-pocketing. This really seemed to impress the lads. I was able to get wallets full of money but I never saw any of the money. My friends would take everything I stole.

Although there was potential for a stable home, the poor character displayed by my family members left me feeling unloved, insecure, isolated and afraid. This feeling was magnified during my early school years by my inability to read and my teacher's inability to teach. I was further isolated through severe bullying. Why would anyone want to remain in that environment?

I was looking for a way out. I knew the path I was taking was wrong but I thought it was the closest thing someone like me was ever going to get to feeling loved, and so I really didn't care about the consequences. I had now found something I was successful at, somewhere I belonged and a place where I was appreciated.

I started to realise we were doing all of this for the money involved, but I didn't see any of it and I didn't know what it was buying. All I knew was that it wasn't being spent on me, and once my friends had it they'd head off for a few hours to spend it without me, leaving me alone at the flat.

I became ever curious, wondering what went on when they disappeared with the money. I began to wonder if I was just being used and if they really cared what happened to me. I finally came to the conclusion that if I was to be truly accepted – part of the family, one of the lads – and have them invite me to go with them to spend the money, then I needed to put all of my energy into impressing them with the biggest theft, the most outrageous escape. I was living to feel accepted and loved and was learning more dangerous ways to earn it.

Chapter 2

The First Time

My life was becoming more and more dangerous. With every theft the probability of getting caught became greater, but I was desperate to be invited with my friends to do whatever it was they did when I was left alone.

My curiosity began to obsess me and tension began to mount between my associates and me. I began to confront them about the issue, questioning their behaviour and my social status in our group. Why should I steal all this stuff for them? What's my reward? It caused a lot of friction, felt most by Ben. There would be blazing rows and they would often come to blows because of my arguments.

One cold Autumn's morning, when I was eight

years old, I set off from Ben's flat to Mum's house for bacon butties. Mum's house was always two degrees hotter than the equator and the smell of bacon and coffee lingered in the hall. A sense of safety rested upon me; I was home. It was here that I could pretend to be a child again; play with toys, have a cuddle with Mum and just rest. Living away for most of the week took its toll. The fast pace of criminal lifestyle was exhilarating but exhausting. As I rested I started thinking more and more about how, even here in the safe place, I still felt like an outsider. I longed to be accepted by my friends. Little did I know my desire was soon to become a reality.

Dad arrived home shortly after that from another long stint overseas and I was shipped back to Ben's flat so that Mum and Dad could spend some time together. On the walk over I started to think about the bullies at school and the spiteful words they'd said. I began to relive in my mind the fights I'd had. All the feelings of being unloved, isolated, angry and fearful surfaced again. As the rain trickled down my hood and ran down my face I scurried through the estate, past the park and arrived at the flat. Ben seemed vacant, like he wasn't really there. I asked if he was okay, but he just grunted a response and invited me in. All the lads were there. I didn't know it at the time but they had all been smoking heroin and cannabis, and an array of bodies littered the living room floor. There was burnt tin foil everywhere and a musky smell filled the room.

I asked what they were doing. Ben tried to explain but in the end gave up. I was given a hand-rolled cigarette and told to try it for myself. Not wanting to let the lads down, I lit the cigarette and smoked it down to the 'roach', the small piece of folded card in the end. It was the first time I had smoked anything other than tobacco. I was eight years old and had just smoked cannabis for the first time. I soon passed out and drifted in and out of consciousness. I was light-headed and felt sick but, at the same time, I was aware that all the negative feelings, the fears and the need to feel loved, had disappeared. This lasted for around twenty minutes.

As I came round from this intoxicated state Ben seemed very worried about me, but all I remember is feeling that I had found what I was missing. I wanted more!

I had finally been accepted as one of the lads. I was invited along to spend the money we'd stolen and I would spend my share on cannabis. This started as a weekend activity and I loved going to Ben's flat knowing now that I could escape the sad reality of my existence for a short while. It was a place where nothing really mattered anymore. Soon I started smoking cannabis throughout the week as well as the weekend. The amount and frequency with which I smoked increased, and the time spent in the realm of reality became less and less as I sought oblivion.

Within three months I was smoking cannabis every day. I now needed it to function in society without anxiety. I also became dependant on crime to provide the income I needed to buy the amount of cannabis that I wanted to smoke. Now they say cannabis is not physically addictive but the psychological dependency I was experiencing at age eight was ruthless. My peers would jeer at me saying, "Look out, it's Luke. Eight years old and an addict." I really didn't care; just light me up and I'll disappear again.

Before I knew it, two years had passed in an intoxicated haze of cannabis-fuelled crime, and I was beginning to lose myself. I had escaped the feelings of being unloved, angry, isolated and afraid but I had also escaped childhood.

Things, however, were about to change. My father got a new job which meant he would work solely in the UK from Monday to Friday. It also meant we had to move from Portsmouth to Bristol. I resented this move. Sure, we would all be together at last, but what about my friends? How would I get drugs in a big city with no one to help me? I will never forget the sinking feeling I had as boxes were packed around me. I remember holding on to my bedroom door-frame, stretched horizontal as my father prised away my grip. I cried the entire two hours to Bristol.

Chapter 3

The Party Drugs

When we arrived in Bristol we found out the house we were due to move into wasn't ready and we would need to live temporarily in an area called Fishponds. It was two weeks until school was due to start and, having spent very little time in education in Portsmouth, I was nervous to say the least. I was in a new area with no friends and no access to drugs. I felt vulnerable, exposed, frightened and anxious. The two weeks sped past quickly and before I knew it I was in my new secondary school, not knowing anyone and struggling to understand what everyone was saying. The only accent I knew was a Pompey one!

The first year at secondary school was not a

pleasant experience for me. I was still very short for my age, with bad eczema and no friends and, to add to this, I spoke differently to everyone else. I couldn't read or write and I was put into the lowest set. The other students ridiculed me. I would constantly get into fights, was isolated and remained friendless. The only thing that kept me in school was the fourteen-mile journey from home. The school was in the middle of nowhere and my mother would drive us there everyday as there was no bus service. If not for this, I would definitely have stopped going. In the last month of the school term, a boy from London called James started at the school. His parents had just moved to Bristol and he was in the same boat as me. We got on well and he was really clever. A friend at last! He would help me with my school work and tried to teach me to read. We had something else in common, though, aside from our different accents. He also smoked cannabis. He lived near to me in Fishponds and he knew where to get hold of the drug. I was off again! After almost a year without any substance abuse I picked up exactly where I had left off, smoking the same amount on a daily basis. There was one difference, though; my new friend had lots of money so I didn't have to steal to fund the habit anymore.

The effects of cannabis soon became insufficient to meet my need for oblivion. My tolerance to cannabis was so high that even if I smoked it all day it would not even scratch the surface of my underlying itch to disappear. The same could be said for my friend so we sought a new high with pills. At the age of eleven I started to take ecstasy. It was great, but very short lived. Ecstasy just wasn't for me, so I went on a hunt for what was. I took acid, LSD, magic mushrooms, amphetamine, poppers, solvents. If it was a drug, I would try it. Then I found it, that thing I needed to get through life without being actually present: cocaine! I loved the stuff. I was alert, exhilarated and could concentrate. I was able to stay awake for days on end and I was completely comfortable with the new me. I was confident, started to talk to girls and, contrary to the first year of school, I was now the life and soul of any party. I also became the go-to guy for a variety of drug cocktails, a new way that my friend and I had found to fund the ever-increasing cost of our habit.

By the age of twelve I was snorting cocaine on a daily basis, completely dependent on its toxic charm. The price tag of my habit had now reached around £40 a day so I had to start practicing some old tricks to fund it. I was shoplifting and pick-pocketing, and James and I would sell cigarettes and cannabis along with whatever we could steal. It was now me who was teaching James. We had learnt that to buy in bulk was much cheaper so we would steal cars to go and collect large quantities of drugs at a time. This, however, put us in contact with some very dodgy people who would give us drugs to sell. We were advised of an amount of money we were expected to make from these drugs, and anything we earned on top was ours to keep. This fast-paced life once more took me away from education but not completely, as I realised that there was a large customer base within the school.

During that time my father's job had fallen through, again because of alcohol abuse. He then seemed to give up on life and focus all his attention on drinking, leaving my mother to work three jobs to keep a roof over our heads. Their relationship turned violent and many times the police were called out until, one day, after my father had hit her, my mother tried to flee in the car but ran him over in the process. The police were called and my father was removed from the home. Within a few months they were divorced, and my father left for the States to start over again.

With my parents out the way, I was even more free to do as I pleased. I would stay out for days at a time, using and selling drugs. I was out of control but I didn't care. My tolerance for cocaine was increasing and no matter how much I used, even to the point of overdose, it still did not have the desired effect. I overdosed on cocaine several times between the ages of twelve and thirteen. Once again I had become discontent with the lack of escape; once again I was having to deal with those old emotions of feeling unloved, isolated, angry and fearful and now, on top of all this, I had to contend with the guilt and shame that comes with living a life of crime.

I began looking for something more, something

to fill the void. I didn't want heroin; I'd seen what that did to my friends in Portsmouth. I wanted something that made me feel awake, alert and alive.

Chapter 4

Crack

Time, as it does, went on. I continued using cocaine and engaging in much of the same behaviour. I became more and more dissatisfied with the results of taking these drugs. I was putting in more effort to get cocaine than ever before yet experiencing less and less of a high.

I was now thirteen years old and the past three years had sped by me. I had been physically there but not really present. Because I lived closer to our dealer's house, James would often give me his money so I could go and buy enough drugs for the week in one go. They never did last the week but that's how we justified spending so much money.

One day, I headed out for my dealer's house. He was someone you didn't want to have as an enemy. I got near the house and noticed two men standing at the doorway. I had never seen them before but they looked menacing. Still, I had come with a purpose and nothing was going to stop me going in. I squeezed past them as they gave me the nod to go in, and walked down the hall past another man who was clearly off his face on something. There was a damp musky smell and it was pitch black as I entered the living room. This was strange as it was midday in the middle of summer and around twenty-seven degrees outside. My dealer was on the sofa, the curtains were duct-taped to the wall to keep the light out and he was sitting there wearing sunglasses, a pipe in hand, in complete darkness. This was weird to say the least, but I asked for my usual concoction of cocaine, cannabis and pills.

As his friends prepared my order I asked him why he was sitting in the dark. He responded saying, "It makes it better!" and showed me his pipe.

I asked, "Makes what better?"

He said, "You can't have this, Luke. The problem

with this is, you'd love it!"

I thought to myself, 'If I'd love it, why can't I have it?' I asked him for a go on his pipe but he got angry and told me to take my stuff and leave. I took the sack of drugs and stormed out of his house. I was angry; I had never been denied drugs before in this place. I'd realised what it was that they were smoking so I went to his competitor three blocks over to get this thing that I would apparently love.

I was thirteen years old when I first smoked crack cocaine. I walked into the crack house in a brand new tracksuit, expensive trainers, over £200 in cash and a bag of drugs with a street value of £2,000. I emerged two weeks later wearing an old pair of shorts and with nothing else. I'd sold my trainers and tracksuit, I'd sold my drugs and all my friend's drugs, and spent all my cash. You see, my dealer had told the truth: I did love it. It was exactly what I needed to blot out reality. I realised however that I had gone to a new extreme with this one and said to myself that, as awesome as the experience was, I wouldn't do it again for a while. I was worried about how to tell James that £1,000 of his money had been spent and I had nothing to show for it. With that, a thought entered my head and I stole a screwdriver from a local shop and robbed the till. But then I went straight back to the crack house not two hours after leaving it and spent it all on more crack.

I was hooked to crack cocaine from the first puff. It was exhilarating; I was wide-awake, everything sped up and I loved the escape it gave me. This was the first drug that scared me because of the power it instantly had over me, but wow, what a feeling it gave me. I could smoke up to £200 worth of crack in a day.

I went back to using my usual cocktail of cocaine, pills and cannabis, only now I would leave some money aside to treat myself once a week to a blow-out on crack. The rest of the time I was becoming more and more like a mad scientist, blending a bit of this and a bit of that to feel a certain way, to party a certain way. The line between reality and fantasy was so blurred that I didn't know where I was most of the time. But one thing I did know was that crack was calling to me. Its voice was the loudest, and its draw the strongest. I knew how Gollum felt in the *Lord of the Rings* films: crack was my 'Precious'. I was trying hard now to keep it to one day a week, but I would too often fold like a cheap paper towel and go smoke crack instead of my usual drugs. I keep saying 'my usual drugs' but at this point crack was becoming my usual drug. Some would call it my drug of choice. I called it home!

Chapter 5

A Downward Spiral

As I continued to chase after the crack high, the periods of not using substances became less and less frequent. Everything seemed to speed up, including the downward spiral of my physical, mental and emotional state.

I was now hearing voices and hallucinating and the only reprieve from this madness was to smoke more crack. Every time the high wore off, the physical and mental symptoms of addiction became apparent, and so I made a decision not to come down – ever! I started to smoke crack every day with no breaks and in ever-increasing amounts. I became so thin and weak from malnutrition that I could no longer steal to fund my habit. I could barely walk. A local drug dealer threw me a lifeline; he gave me large quantities of crack to sell and anything I earned over what he wanted back was mine to fund my own habit. The problem was that I wasn't able to make enough money to feed my addiction so eventually, when I was given £3,000 of crack to sell, I smoked it all myself. The dealer was furious and he was not the sort of person to let something like this go. I went on the run but I soon found out just how much trouble I was in.

I spent the next six months living on the streets and sofa-surfing in Bristol, London, Leeds and Glasgow. My health continued to worsen and I was having to fix on cheaper alternatives. But the problem was I had become so tolerant to these substances that they did little for me now. I was running from some very nasty people, and was psychotic as a result of drug use. I couldn't escape the sense of paranoia. I would wake every morning in withdrawal, desperately looking to see if I had any drugs left, or any money, and trying to plan how to get more. I would need to drink alcohol or cough medicine just to function enough to get myself to a dealer's house to buy more drugs. This wasn't fun, not what I signed up for. It wasn't working and somewhere in all of this I had lost my ability to choose something different. I was in trouble but couldn't stop. I moved back to Bristol and all was well for a while. I knew many people who would get me what I wanted so I could continue to use.

One night I found out just how much trouble I was in! It was mid Winter and I was walking home. I was under-dressed and cold, withdrawing and looking for someone to give me the drug I needed to fix me. I walked through the pitch-black streets with the rain dripping down my face and saturating my clothes, past the newsagents, and there they were: a group of twenty men with bits of wood, metal poles, stones and bats. I recognised one man as the dealer I had ripped off. My heart was beating at a million miles an hour. I started to run, my lungs feeling like they would explode. My legs were weak but I was desperate to get away. I think I got about fifty yards before they caught and surrounded me. I dodged the first punch but the second landed hard on my face, immediately followed by something hard crunching into the back of my skull. Everything went black. The next thing I remember, I was in an ambulance drifting in and out of consciousness. I remember thinking, 'Just let me die, I've had enough of this life.'

I woke up in intensive care three weeks later. My injuries consisted of broken ribs, nose, wrist and ankle, a fractured skull, and extensive bruising to my face and body. A doctor advised me that, although I had survived the beating, if I carried on doing drugs I would be dead in six months. I had a scarred liver and my one working kidney was failing. I was only sixteen years old.

The police informed me that the incident had been caught on CCTV. I wanted to see, as I couldn't remember a thing. The hard thing that had knocked me out was a scaffolding bar. They had carried me unconscious to a phone box and slammed the door repeatedly into my head. They stamped on my head and ribs and kicked me everywhere. I had lain there lifeless for over thirty minutes until a dog walker stumbled across me and called an ambulance.

In the month and a half I stayed in hospital, I had not one visitor. I discharged myself and went straight out to buy some crack, still battered and bruised and giving myself six months to live. I honestly thought to myself that I would just smoke crack until I died. I tried to hang myself to speed up the process but the bolt I tied myself to came out of the ceiling. I couldn't even kill myself properly.

A couple of weeks later I overdosed in a crack house in the St Paul's area of Bristol. The people I was with thought I was dead so they took what little I had left and threw me into a skip, covering me with a mouldy mattress. I woke up a few hours later and carried on smoking. Nothing but death could separate me from this slavery to addiction.

My absolute rock bottom, though, was when my mother and sister, who I hadn't seen in three years, walked past me as I was begging at Bristol Temple Meads train station. I was five-and-a-half stone in weight, and my own mother didn't even recognise me! My sister recognised only my eyes and nose and said, "Mum, I think that's Luke."

Only as my mother laid her eyes on me and our gazes met did she recognise me. I have never felt so ashamed in all my life. I got up and slipped off into an alleyway. Walking past a shop window I saw my reflection: what had I become? I tried to stop using for real this time. I lasted just four hours – four hours was all I had in my own strength before I couldn't hack it anymore and lit up. I weighed practically nothing, was psychotic, had liver and kidney failure, and still I couldn't stop.

Chapter 6

The Turning Point

I had reached an all-time low, and had failed to stop using – I felt useless, powerless and worthless. I was determined, however, to sort this out. I tried again, and stayed clean for two days; tried again and lasted for three days. Eventually, after two months, I managed two weeks clean. The audible and visual hallucinations where horrific. I couldn't sleep, eat or function. I didn't want to use but, on the other hand, one blast on a crack pipe and it all disappeared. I was doing what I no longer desired to do. I might as well be dead, I thought.

I made up my mind that if I was going to die anyway then I might as well do it without the aggravation of being drug-free and crazy! It was early evening, and I headed out to score. As I was passing a church, a man walked out and lit up a cigarette. I remember thinking what a hypocrite he was but that didn't stop me from walking up to him and asking him for one. I was skinny as a rake, covered in vomit and had messed my pants. He gave me a cigarette and asked my name. Now I'm not sure why I said this but the following words came tumbling out of my mouth almost uncontrollably: "My name's Luke. I'm a crack addict and I need help."

The man laughed at me, walked up the steps of the church, turned back around and said, "You comin' in then?"

I was furious. 'Nobody laughs at me', I thought, 'Yes I'm coming in, and you're getting stabbed.' He had walked off into the church and I stormed after him only to find a hall full of elderly ladies. There was no sign of him anywhere. One of the women asked if I was OK. I just laughed, thinking, 'Do I look okay to you?'

The women surrounded me and manhandled me into a chair. My knuckles were white inside my pocket as I gripped my flick-knife. I was given a cup of tea and a generous plate of biscuits. All the time, though, my eyes roamed to and fro across the room. There were people wearing nice suits and sweet perfume, all sat neatly in their seats, and musicians practising up front before the service, but no sign of this guy. He had disappeared without a trace.

I was beginning to relax and thought I'd just finish the tea and leave. The music started to play as the service started. The very idea of Jesus and Christianity seemed foolish to me. After all, dead people don't get up! What a stupid belief. Then the man from outside walked out onto the stage. I could feel my heart begin to race as I remembered him laughing at me. This was escalated and exacerbated by my psychotic paranoia. All I needed was an opportunity. I'd stab him and run, but not in front of all these people. I decided to wait until the end of the service and then I'd get him in the crowd and slip away into the night.

He began to speak, something about him being baptised. I didn't really get it, but then he started to talk about his life. As he talked, I was less and less able to block out what he was saying. He had been addicted to heroin, and then he talked about this person who had saved his life. He didn't name the person until the end, when he said the person who had saved him was called Jesus Christ. Some others there put him in a big bathtub thing, pushed his head under the water and the people in the church went wild, clapping and singing as the music started up again. I didn't want religion or Jesus but I didn't want to use again, and if this guy could stop, then just maybe he could help me. I couldn't leave now and I certainly couldn't stab him.

I plucked up the courage to go and speak to him, pushing through the crowd of ridiculously happy people to get to him. I said, "Can you help me? Please, man, you've got to help me!"

He said, "Okay, but you have to do exactly as I say." I responded, "I'll do anything!"

He told me that I was to go home with him, that he had a spare room at his parents' place and they wouldn't mind. This was all a little bit surreal, but I was so desperate that I agreed. He took me home and I was introduced to his mum and dad and had the best meal I'd eaten in months! I was told that, in order to stay off drugs, I would need to finish withdrawing, and for my own safety they would lock me in the spare room. I was shocked but I agreed. The next three days were hell on earth. I tossed and turned, hallucinated, cried, screamed, tore the room apart and punched holes in the door and walls. I was brought a meal three times a day. When I passed out I'd often wake up with someone mopping my brow and praying. I got through it by some miracle and was invited to the family table to eat dinner with them. I still had audible hallucinations and was very weak. They introduced themselves properly and I found out his name was also Luke. The next morning Luke came to my room with loads of tools. I was to learn to plaster and paint in order to fix the mess I'd made of the room. I was very shaky and anxious. I was still obsessing over drugs and had furiously strong cravings. Luke and his family decided to keep me in the house for a few weeks until the cravings had died down. I was then to go everywhere Luke went.

Luke was doing lots of voluntary work with the church and so this was where I spent a lot of my time. I would never stay for the meetings as I didn't believe in God and didn't really want to, either. I would sit on the steps outside, smoking cigarettes until the meetings were over. After a couple of months I was offered a space in a local dry house. I also started to do voluntary work with the church's homeless team one day a week. I kept this up, but the cravings remained and I was obsessing over drugs for the majority of each day. I was in and out of the hospital for tests on my kidneys, and assessments with the mental health team, as I was still hearing voices and had severe anxiety. I was off illegal drugs but had to daily take more tablets than I'd ever taken whilst using. I was a shell. Drugs were ninety-nine per cent of who I had become and, now they had been removed, I no longer knew who I was. I was terrified but determined to get through without using. After six months of being clean I was still in the same condition as when I started detox.

Chapter 7

Meeting Jesus

I was sat with Luke in a park one Sunday afternoon, waiting for the evening service to start. I had begun attending the church by this time, just as a safeguard really. If I went to church, Luke could keep an eye on me. Luke leaned over and said, "You do realise that if you don't accept Jesus, you're going to relapse, right?", and without even thinking I answered, "Yes."

Luke then asked how I felt about this, stating, "This is the most honest you've ever been."

I responded, "I'm terrified, the last time I was clean for this long and relapsed it took me three years to get clean again. My body doesn't have that long. If I use, I'm signing my death certificate and

I am terrified of dying."

"Why won't you accept Jesus, then?" he asked.

I thought about this for a minute. I had seen some weird stuff during my time using drugs. Some of the African dealers I would hang about with were witch doctors and others were into witchcraft. I had seen tables and chairs move about on their own when these individuals entered or left a room. I could believe people being healed and water turned to wine – after all, TV magicians were all the rage then. You see, it was not the miracles that made Jesus seem like a fairy tale; I was simply unable to get my head around this Jesus dying and coming back to life. It just seemed too out there, so I answered, saying, "You can't come back to life when you die! I could believe if it weren't for that. Being raised from the dead – it's a fairy tale."

I was left knowing relapse was inevitable, that I was just clinging onto being clean to preserve my life for as long as possible. I would not wish this state of limbo on my worst enemy. In the world of Alcoholics Anonymous I was what they call a 'dry drunk' – nothing had changed except I wasn't using anymore.

After church that night, Luke walked me home. When we arrived he asked to pray for me and I accepted his offer. When he finished he said, "Oh, by the way, I know you like to challenge stuff. Try reading the book of Romans and prove it wrong." He knew me well. I would question anything and fight anything he suggested regarding God.

I said, "Alright then, but it'll be a shame to shatter your faith when I prove this is all make-believe." He laughed and walked off into the night.

I had a Bible but had never read it. Firstly, I thought it was a load of rubbish and, secondly, I couldn't read! Two weeks later Luke asked, "You're not reading Romans, are you?"

I replied saying, "How did you know?"

"Because you've not asked a single question yet. You normally question everything" he answered.

I had to come clean and tell him that I couldn't read, which led to him teaching me to read as we went through the book of Romans together. He was right – I had a million and one questions about it all. Then one day we were reading through Romans chapter 7 and I read these words: "For the good that I will to do, I do not do; but the evil I will not to do, that I practice" (Romans 7:19). I stopped reading immediately, completely astounded. Wasn't this describing me? I wanted to live a new way but always found myself living the old way.

I went home that night perplexed to think that this Bible was talking to me. I started reading that evening on my own and read Romans 8:1: "There is therefore now no condemnation for those who are in Christ Jesus, who do not walk according to the flesh, but according to the Spirit." I thought, 'No more condemnation sounds good!'

It was Romans 8:38-39 that really got me, though. As I read "For I am persuaded that neither death nor life, nor angels nor principalities nor powers, nor things present nor things to come, nor height nor depth, nor any other created thing, shall be able to separate us from the love of God which is in Christ Jesus our Lord", I was beaten. I couldn't fault this book. Romans chapter 7 had me realising that these words were changing me, and Romans chapter 8 left me wanting Jesus. I got on my knees and prayed for the first time: "God, I don't have you worked out, I still don't know how you can rise from the grave, but I believe you are speaking to me through this book. If you take the obsession I have to use, or the craving I have for crack, I will fight the other and follow you for the rest of my life."

I felt no different, as if I was talking to my bedroom wall, so I went to bed feeling rather foolish.

I woke the next morning and instantly felt like something was wrong, although I couldn't tell you what. I just didn't feel right. I had to go to church as it was my day to volunteer in the soup kitchen. I went full of anxiety. What was wrong with me? This praying stuff clearly hadn't worked. I was feeling worse than ever.

The people at church knew instantly that something was bothering me. They too became concerned for me. They knew my history and were probably wondering if today was the day I would relapse. I managed to muscle through to lunchtime without talking to anyone too much. No sooner did the clock tick twelve o'clock than I was off, scurrying down the road thinking, 'What's the point? I'm off to go use.'

I hurried over the road and crossed into the

park, and then it happened! I noticed the colour of the grass, the smell of the flowers and the sound of the birds, the gentle breeze across my face. It was at that moment that I stepped out of the black-and-white movie that my life had become and into the fullness of God's creation. I realised the feeling that I thought something was wrong was because I had not had a single audible hallucination all day – the voices had gone. I felt well in myself, it had just taken me half a day to realise it. It had worked! God had healed me physically, psychologically and spiritually. I knew it in my heart. God had removed all cravings and obsessions and I hadn't even realised for half the day!

I rushed back to tell the others from the church. "I've met Jesus and He has healed me," I shouted across the lunch hall! An older man named John, who led the Alpha course, took me into a smaller room and I told him everything. He was over the moon with excitement for me. We prayed and he called Luke to come.

In the weeks that followed I got better and better. I was positively discharged from the mental health team with no more need for medication but it was my visit to the hospital that was the most astounding. I had gone into the hospital for a full scan to check up on all the damage my body had sustained during the beating I'd received. Also, if you'll remember from the beginning of my story, I mentioned an undiagnosed kidney infection I'd had as a baby that had left me with one kidney smaller than the other and which didn't function very well. Through my drug use I had damaged the good kidney and had been told I needed a transplant. After the scan, the doctor came out looking perplexed.

I asked, "Is everything okay, Doc?"

The doctor advised, "Everything is better than okay, Mr Selway. I have to apologise, but I've never seen anything like this. Your kidneys are the same size on this scan and both are fully functional. We will need to do some extra checks to be certain, but this is nothing short of a miracle." I was then prodded and poked until all tests confirmed I had been healed! I was discharged from all areas of the health care service, fit and well. I had met Jesus and He had healed me!

Chapter 8

New Life

I was now attending church during the week, serving on the homeless outreach team twice a week, at Alpha once a week, as well as attending both Sunday services. I was studying the Bible and praying, meeting with other Christians and asking loads of questions to further my understanding. I was passionate and excited about the change in me. I was so interested and wanted to learn everything I could about this Jesus who had saved me. Twelve months passed in the blink of an eye. I was walking with God and learning more and more about who I was called to be!

It wasn't all great, though. Around this time a local dealer had found out where I was living and started to post drugs through the letter box. This went on for a while and things became really nasty as threats started to be posted as well. I owed this guy money, and he wanted me to start using so he could order me about once more, like his puppet on a string. I didn't give in, though, and he got annoyed, making threats on my life. This guy was not to be messed with. I had heard rumours that he had cut off someone's hand for stealing from him. As time went on these threats became more frequent and more severe. My family, with whom I had re-established contact and who now trusted me again, decided that I should move back to Portsmouth to live with my grandparents. With the dry-house manager's help, my granddad drove up at two o'clock in the morning to spirit me away so no one would know where I had gone. I was so happy to be back in Portsmouth. My granddad told me that, while I stayed with him, I was either to go to college (and he would pay for it) or I was to get a job. The thought of college was daunting so I decided to get a job. One week later I started work in a warehouse loading lorries. The one downside was that I worked Sundays and so couldn't get to church. It took only three months of not going to church before I started to think about drugs again. 'Just once,' I thought, 'You'll be okay this time, and no one will find out.' The list of justifications was vast. I quickly recognised that I was entering dangerous territory and so quit the job. I applied to do engineering at college and got accepted on condition that I passed a Maths and English exam.

I started going to a Baptist church in Portsmouth. I just turned up one night at six-thirty in the evening, thinking that must be when all churches had their evening service. I will never forget that day: I was welcomed by a young lady called Flic, and invited to the building next door as it was a more contemporary service for young adults. I was greeted there by a guy called Shaun. We were to become very close friends in the coming months. I loved the teaching and just sat in to learn more and more about the things of God. I was mentored by a man named Dave who helped me when it came to spiritual giftings such as speaking in tongues, like they did in Acts chapter 2. I was studying and doing well, enjoying church and learning more about God, and loving living with Nan and Gramps.

I passed my engineering course and celebrated two years clean, and then met a girl in church who I really liked. We started to date but I very quickly realised that I was not at all ready for this type of relationship. The relationship ended badly, which was my fault. I said and did things in the worst way possible to push this girl away so she wouldn't see my pain. I was still very immature in this area. I became complacent in my walk with God and started to move from church to church, not really finding anywhere that I wanted to commit to. This led to me beginning to walk away from God. I started clubbing two or three nights of the week with a friend who also had one foot in the church and one in the world. Jesus speaks of this in Revelation 3:16 saying, "So then, because you are lukewarm, and neither cold nor hot, I will vomit you out of My mouth."

I was in a dangerous place and about to get a wake-up call. I went to the toilet of a club one night and was offered a line of cocaine. I almost accepted! The Bible explains in Psalm 139:7-10 that there is nowhere we can go to hide from God. I thank God that even in that place His Spirit convicted me then and there and I was able to refuse the drug. I ran up to my friend and said, "I gotta get out of here, and I'm never clubbing again. You coming?" He said no but I left anyway. I have not stepped foot in a club since that day.

I decided to get serious, but had no church to go to. I started to study God's Word on my own and also started to pray again. I admitted to God my wrongdoing and turned to face the other way. This is called repentance.

Chapter 9

Family Church

In all my struggling, God had kept me from using. I realised that this walk with God was not easy, nor did it mean all my troubles would disappear. Life is still life; the difference is that with God I have His strength to draw on when I have none. Matthew 11:28 says, "Come to Me, all you who labour and are heavy laden, and I will give you rest." God had helped me through and I was now almost five years clean.

Some friends suggested that I go to Family Church, a large church with a congregation in the Buckland area of Portsmouth. I didn't think this was a good idea, as I felt it would be easy for me to get lost in a crowd, but I really wanted to find a church! I got up early one Sunday morning and began to drive around Portsmouth looking for a church. Every one I drove to unsettled my spirit. I must have driven to every church but Family Church. It got to be past the time church started so I began to drive home. I passed the front entrance of a school and saw the banners for Family Church – they met in the school each week. The banner showed that there were two morning services, the second of which was about to start. The conviction of the Holy Spirit was so overpowering that I obeyed and went in. What I was about to experience would change my life again!

Let me start by saying that this was no ordinary church. For a start they had lighting rigs, smoke machines, a massive stage, multimedia and a sports hall full of people who were expectant on God! Then the band leader shouted out, "Good morning, church. Let's jump to our feet; it's time to praise God!" The band started to play and the people started to jump up and down. I found myself involuntarily joining in. It was like a rave from my drug days, only I was drunk in the Holy Spirit. After worship we were welcomed by a very bubbly character called Steu, one of the pastors of the church, who said, "If there's anyone here for the first time, we want to welcome you. We have a gift for you. Please raise your hand and one of the hosting team will bring it to you." I raised my hand and was given a yellow bag that said 'Welcome to Church'; inside was information about the church and its events. The message was brought by the senior pastor of the church, Andy Elmes, and it was about the vision of Family Church to serve its community – and I was game!

After the service I was ushered round to a large coffee hall and lots of people came to say hello. I was like one of the family. This church was exactly as it was called; a big family. I was told there was another congregation in Havant, about seven miles away, that was meeting in the evening and so I decided to go. It was the same experience as in the morning but on a smaller scale. It was here that I spoke to Pastor Steu and was invited to go later that week for a coffee and breakfast with him.

I spent some of the breakfast meeting explaining what had led up to me being at the church and Steu, in turn, told me about their internship programme. The Family Church Internship consisted of three days a week voluntary work within the church, serving in every team, and being subsidised to do a two-year Bible college course. I wasn't sure about this as I was earning a good wage in engineering at this point and had just moved into my own apartment, but I agreed to think about it.

I arrived at church the next week at seven in the morning to help with their set up. As it was in a school, the team had to build the stage, lighting system, sound and media, coffee hall, and kids' church rooms before the first service started. I then stayed for both services and helped pack everything away afterwards. It was amazing – I wasn't just a spectator anymore, I was serving God! I was part of a team that made church happen and enabled people to meet with Jesus for the first time. What a privilege!

I was invited to a home group run by a man named Glynn, who also headed up the homeless outreach team. Glynn was then, and still is, one of the most humble, generous and understanding men I have ever met. The more I went to the home group, the more God was impressing on my heart that I should do the internship. I was terrified. How would I pay my rent? What if I couldn't do it? The list went on. Just as I was coming to a decision about the internship I was offered a massive promotion at work. It was so enticing, but how could I ignore what I felt God was saying after all He had done?

Chapter 10

Internship

The more I struggled with the decision of stepping out in faith to do an internship that would leave me over £25,000 a year worse off, the more God provoked a side of me that loves an adventure. I was walking home one evening, praying about what to do, and I walked past a local drug and alcohol rehabilitation centre. I decided to go in and ask if they had a vacancy that would allow me the flexibility to do the internship. That very morning a support worker had left, giving no notice, and they were struggling to cover shifts. I had a twenty-minute chat and was offered the job. I handed in my notice at work the next morning and went to work as a recovery support worker.

I signed up for the internship, was interviewed and accepted, even though I was described by one of the interviewers as 'rough round the edges'.

Trying to juggle the three days a week doing the internship with the night shifts in the rehab was not easy, and there were days I would not turn up at the church office because I'd overslept. I would be given book reports to do that I would hand in late. Basically, I was not doing so well as an intern. I was trying hard but the harder I tried the more things seemed to go against me. I would speak before thinking and was teased by the office receptionist that I had no 'filter'. She would also tell me to go back outside and come back in when I'd told my face it was saved – in other words, come back in when I'd learnt how to smile!

I was really struggling with internship but then I started to realise I was looking for praise from people for what I was doing. What I was beginning to learn was that if you look for the praises of men for doing the work of God and you don't get it, you lose motivation. I learnt that God sees what we do in the background and He rewards us for it. Things became a little easier when I understood this. Every facet of my character was challenged under great leadership during internship and I learned a lot.

The church had an annual retreat for men over a weekend on the Isle of Wight and, as an intern, I got to go free as I was serving throughout. It was incredible. Every day we had meetings, worship and shared stories, as well as golf, table tennis and football. It was on the second day there that I went for some quiet time on my own on a cliff top overlooking the sea. Having learned that it's better to serve than to be served, I asked God what I could do for Him. God answered by showing me a vision of a Christian drug and alcohol treatment centre. At the end of the next meeting we were invited to share what God had been saying to us and I got up and shared a little bit of my story, rough edges and all, and what God had shown me. Listening to my story was a guy called Steve, who had just finished a diploma in Christian counselling but didn't know where it would lead him. Steve came alongside my vision and partnered with me from that day.

I scraped through that first year of internship, graduating by the skin of my teeth. I had started to have prayer meetings with Steve, and a few others had joined us. We were at the planning stages – how would this vision get started? God had told me we would have a property in two years but others believed it would take five at least. I ignored these comments as I was fast learning that God's Word carries greater truth than any situation or circumstance.

I decided to do the second year of internship and set up the Christian rehab as a new ministry as part of the programme. I started the year much more mature, both spiritually and emotionally. Romans 12:2 says, "And do not be conformed to this world, but be transformed by the renewing of your mind, that you may prove what is that good and acceptable and perfect will of God." It was the combination of good leadership and discipleship, coupled with a new focus on God's Word and His calling on my life, that was taking me further into relationship with Jesus. I started to understand the character of God and that enabled me to begin to imitate Jesus.

I did find it difficult to get the balance right, however, between internship duties, work and the rehab ministry we now called Inside Out. Because of this, I wasn't going to be able to graduate the internship programme. I was devastated but I decided to ask to carry on with the internship regardless. I set a goal to graduate in the sight of God and Him alone! Despite this, watching the other interns graduate was difficult as I knew I could have done better. But I remember what my mentor said: "Are you willing to do it even when no one gives credit? It's all about character; it's the depth of a man's character that supports the height of his vision." I was now willing to have God break me and build me for His purposes.

Chapter 11

Inside Out

So Inside Out was birthed during my second year of internship and was established under the umbrella of the charity called Empower Global (Family Church). During the first year of my internship, when I received the vision from God to set up a Christian rehab in Portsmouth, a few other people caught hold of the vision, and we would meet once a month to pray. The timeframe for things to take off, I believed, would be two years. The team of people around me didn't think that this was realistic and advised it could be more like five years before we had an actual property. I decided to be open to their advice but I would stand on what God had said.

As we journeyed on, I noticed people would come and go, their commitment to the vision wavering. Sometimes I would look at the small number of us trying to work towards making the vision a reality and I would feel completely useless and overwhelmed. Nonetheless, it was God Himself who had called me and so I remained consistent and faithful. The prayer team started to grow and I began to connect with other relevant organisations that could help us start the work. At this time I met with a man who had written *The Recovery Course,* a Christian twelve-step programme designed to run once a week for sixteen weeks. He gave me full use of this material so I created a training package that would teach others to run the course. I advertised this training to the local church and had a great response, with sixteen people signing up to do the training. Once these people had completed the training, I advertised *The Recovery Course* to people suffering from addiction and we started our first course from the Family Church offices. This course was a great success and we started to see people who were hopelessly addicted come to find hope in Jesus and walk free from addiction. In all of this there were highs and lows, with many people recovering but some relapsing, even dying. I experienced a roller-coaster ride of every kind of emotion whilst walking with these people whom society had rejected. One thing was starting to bother me, though: the homeless people we worked with experienced real success while on the course, yet when the course was over and done, they would have to go back to the same environment they had come from with little chance of implementing what they had learned. If only we had a house, I thought.

One person I've not mentioned yet is Kudzi, a Zimbabwean woman who volunteered as a receptionist at Family Church on Mondays. I had annoyed Kudzi every Monday over the two years of my internship by asking her "If your mood was a chocolate bar, what chocolate bar would that be?" and other such profound questions. Kudzi mostly ignored me. After my second year had finished, I would book a computer in the office once a week to do work for Inside Out. It was during this time that I began to realise that Kudzi was the most beautiful woman I had ever seen, inside and out. She was a picture of the Proverbs 31 woman to me. I was terrified; the last relationship I'd been in had ended disastrously. My experience showed me that when I started to date, I began to worship the new relationship instead of God. I did what any normal Christian man would do: I prayed for her to find a different church! That way, I reasoned, I wouldn't be distracted from the call of God on my life. I spoke to my mentor about it and he soon put me right, advising me that I shouldn't be praying someone out of the church. I went on trying to ignore the way I was feeling about Kudzi, but the feelings just grew. To cut a long story short we fell in love and started to date, placing God first in every way. Just before we got engaged, Inside Out successfully ran its first Recovery Course, and we were married in May 2012.

I was still working in the treatment centre at this time and was making contact through the centre with people and organisations who had properties to offer Inside Out. None of these options panned out, but then a man named Peter contacted me. He listened to my story and vision and shared a little about the work he had done with ex-offenders and drug addicts. Peter went on to purchase a two-bedroom flat in Portsmouth for Inside Out to manage on his behalf!

We were by now running three Recovery Courses a year and we were starting to see the fruit – people breaking free from addiction, getting saved and attending church. The local treatment services started to refer the people they were helping into our service. Their funding didn't stretch far enough but the care that Inside Out offered was free.

Inside Out was growing, with a prayer team, mentoring team and volunteers to help run the Recovery Course. And then it happened! God revealed more of the vision to me. We had gone to Hull to visit my wife's family, and whilst we were there we attended their church, Millennium Harvest Church, led by two amazing pastors, Hartness and Fungai Samushonga. The church was fasting and praying together and we joined in. After an amazing weekend we returned to Portsmouth, but we both felt called to move to Hull. This was confirmed by a dream and in many other ways, so we decided to be obedient and follow this calling. In order to do that, I needed to get Inside Out Portsmouth to a point where it could be managed locally, and overseen from Hull, where I planned to start another branch of Inside Out. This process involved Inside Out becoming its own charity, training and raising a team in Portsmouth, and a whole lot of faith to once again leave security and exchange it for uncertainty. By this time, my wife had given birth to our son, Judah. The last time I stepped out of employment to be obedient to the call of God, it was just me on my own. I now had to think of my wife and son. What if I'd heard wrong? How was I going to support my family?

Chapter 12

Hull

We moved from Portsmouth to Hull in faith and obedience to God in January 2014, and I was offered a job working as a mental health support worker. Trying to balance family time, my job, setting up a new branch of Inside Out and overseeing the Portsmouth branch seemed impossible at times. To add to this, I was becoming frustrated as things were taking longer than I thought they should to set up Inside Out in Hull. Countless efforts to raise a team seemed to be thwarted by a lack of commitment. God was teaching me to be patient and wait on His timing. We committed once a month to pray about this situation and invited the church to join us. Sometimes we would have a full meeting and sometimes it would just be me. Even when it was only me I would still teach and pray. This sounds odd but I have learnt that if I consistently show up and do what God has told me to do then He does the rest.

I was offered and accepted a job working for the substance misuse team in Doncaster. I commuted one hundred miles a day for nine months until I was promoted to a position in Hull for the same company. At this point we were starting to see a better turnout to our prayer meetings, although there were still occasions when no one else would come. It was at this time that Peter, who had bought the flat in Portsmouth for Inside Out, offered to buy a property for my family to live in at a much lower cost. This gave us the freedom to take a pay cut to work more hours for Inside Out.

****

It is now September 2015 and we have partnered with another charity that purchases properties for charities like us, to help house the homeless. We are on the brink of opening the first property in Hull. We have trained our first seven volunteer mentors and are advertising the first ever Recovery Course in Hull. People have been asking me to write a book for a long time but I would always use my lack of education as an excuse not to try. It is the conviction of the Holy Spirit that has caused me to write these pages.

But this is not the end of the story; there are plenty more chapters to come in the book of my life. God has a vision and a purpose for me.

You may have a relationship with Jesus, be regularly attending church, but what is it that God is calling you to do? It may not be something as complicated as setting up a charity; it may be as simple as serving on a team in church. Let me encourage you to step out, take a chance. At the end of your life, when you're sitting in your rocking chair, what will you regret more – stepping out in faith and risking failure, or not stepping out at all?

You may be reading this and not have a relationship with Jesus. A relationship with Jesus is a free gift. No matter how good or bad your situation, the Bible says that all have fallen short of God's standards, that God is love, yet a perfect Judge. He doesn't want anyone to be punished for sin, but because He is a good Judge He has to punish sin. He solved this dilemma by sending Jesus, who was fully man and fully God, to die in your place to pay for your shortfall. You can only receive Jesus' free gift of grace through faith, which the Bible tells us is the substance of things hoped for, the evidence of things not seen. Faith is not just head knowledge, nor is it something to be used only in a crisis. It is putting our trust in Jesus and enjoy a two-way relationship.

If you're reading this thinking, 'I want what he's got, I would like to enter that relationship with Jesus too,' then please pray this prayer:

> *Jesus, thank You for loving me. I believe that You came to this earth fully man and fully God, that You lived a blameless life and upon the cross became the payment for my sin. I believe that on the third day You rose again, having defeated death and*

the devil. I believe in Your life, death and resurrection. I welcome You into my heart.

Amen.

If you have prayed that prayer and meant it, I am so happy for you. Remember, there is nothing more you need to do to obtain salvation. It is a free gift that you could never have earned and didn't deserve. It's grace. I urge you to tell someone about the decision you've made to follow Jesus, connect with a local church and learn more about who Jesus is.

If you are like I was – struggling with an addiction – or would like to get involved or donate financially to the work of Inside Out, please contact us at **insideout-rehab.org**.

Further Information

For further information about the author of this book, or to order more copies, please contact:

Great Big Life Publishing
Empower Centre
83-87 Kingston Road
Portsmouth
Hampshire
PO2 7DX
United Kingdom
info@greatbiglifepublishing.com

Are you an Author?

Do you have a word from God on your heart that you're looking to get published to a wider audience?

We're looking for manuscripts that identify with our own vision of bringing life-giving and relevant messages to the Body of Christ. Send yours for review towards possible publication to:

Great Big Life Publishing
Empower Centre
83-87 Kingston Road
Portsmouth
Hampshire
PO2 7DX
United Kingdom
info@greatbiglifepublishing.com